Searchlight BOOKS™

How Do
We Use
Money?

Understanding Credit

Carla Mooney

Lerner Publications
Minneapolis

Lerner Publications Company
A division of Lerner Publishing Group, Inc.
241 First Avenue North
Minneapolis, MN 55401 USA

For reading levels and more information, look up this title at www.lernerbooks.com.

Content consultant: Donna Little, Associate Professor of Accounting and Finance, Menlo College

Library of Congress Cataloging-in-Publication Data

Mooney, Carla, 1970–
    Understanding credit / by Carla Mooney.
      pages   cm. — (Searchlight books™—How do we use money?)
    Includes index.
    ISBN 978-1-4677-5229-9 (lib. bdg. : alk. paper)
    ISBN 978-1-4677-6255-7 (EB pdf)
    1. Credit—Juvenile literature. 2. Loans—Juvenile literature. 3. Money—Juvenile literature. I. Title.
HG3701.M656 2015
332.7—dc23
                                        2014022185

Manufactured in the United States of America
1 — BP — 12/31/14

Contents

Chapter 1

CASH AND CREDIT

People use money to buy things they need or want. Sometimes they pay with cash. Other times, they pay with a credit card. These two methods of payment may seem similar. Most stores accept both. However, they are very different.

Kids usually spend and save cash. What is another way to pay that adults sometimes use?

Cash is money you have earned. Adults earn money from their jobs. You might earn money by doing chores at home. Maybe you get paid for babysitting. The money you earn belongs to you. Using coins or paper bills is the simplest way to spend your money.

Credit cards are commonly used for online shopping.

Debit cards and credit cards look the same, but they work very differently.

A debit card is another way to spend money. It is a small plastic card. To use it, you slide the card through a machine at a cash register. The money you spend comes out of your bank account. This means that debit cards let you spend the money you already have. Credit cards are different. They let you use the credit card company's money to pay for things. You must pay the company back later.

Using Credit

Using credit is borrowing money to buy something. You might borrow money from a friend. People also borrow money from banks. A kid might borrow money from a parent for a new bike. Adults might borrow money from a bank to buy a car or a home.

Kids sometimes borrow money from a parent.

Borrowed money is called debt. You promise to pay back the money you borrowed. A bank that lends you money will charge interest. This is money the bank charges you for borrowing its money. Interest is a percentage of your debt. Imagine you owe $100 to a bank. The bank charges 10 percent interest each month. At the end of the month, 10 percent of $100 is added to the debt. This equals $10. Now you owe the bank $110.

A credit card lets you use debt to pay for something. When you use a credit card, you borrow money from a credit card company. You must pay back this money. Credit card companies also charge interest. Interest increases over time. The longer you take to pay back the money, the more you must pay.

You must fill out an application form to get a credit card.

Decision Time

You want to buy the latest shoes. But they cost $60!
How can you get them? You earn $20 walking dogs
each week. Should you save money until you have
enough? Or should you ask a parent for a $60 loan and
buy the shoes right away? Imagine your mom or dad will
charge you $3 interest each week until the debt is paid.

Option #1 – Save and Pay with Cash

Week	Income	Cash
1	$20	$20
2	$20	$40
3	$20	$60

Option #2 – Paying Back Loan from Parents

Week	Income	Cash	Interest	Total Debt
1	$20	$20	$3	$63
2	$20	$40	$6	$66
3	$20	$60	$9	$69
4	$20	$80	$12	$72

What are the advantages of options 1 and 2? What
are the disadvantages? Which option would you
choose, and why?

People use credit cards for different reasons. Some feel that carrying a card is easier than carrying cash. Others need to buy something but do not have enough money. For example, imagine your aunt's car gets a flat tire. She needs to buy a new tire. If she has savings, she can make this purchase. But what if she doesn't have enough cash? She could use a credit card to pay for the tire. Later, she will have to pay the money back. She may have to pay interest too. The total cost could be more than if she had used savings.

Credit cards can be useful for unexpected large expenses, such as car repairs.

EXPENSES PAID MOST OFTEN WITH CREDIT CARDS

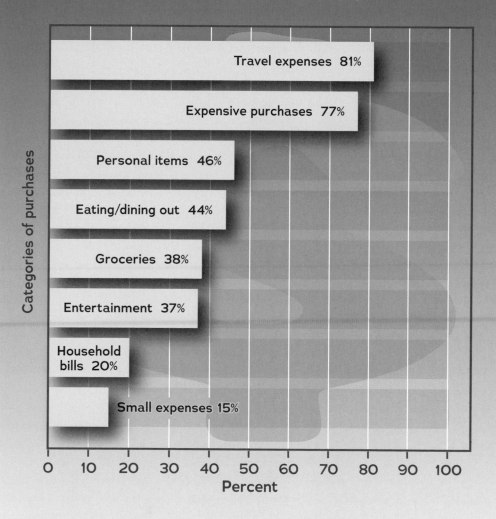

Categories of purchases

Travel expenses 81%

Expensive purchases 77%

Personal items 46%

Eating/dining out 44%

Groceries 38%

Entertainment 37%

Household bills 20%

Small expenses 15%

0   10   20   30   40   50   60   70   80   90   100

Percent

This diagram shows some of the most common things people purchase with credit. For example, 81 percent of travel expenses are paid with credit cards, rather than cash. Why might people use credit so often for travel expenses? Why do people use credit cards for small expenses less often?

People usually need to visit a bank and meet with a banker to take out a loan.

Credit cards are not the only way to use credit. Loans are also credit. Banks loan customers money. Then the customers pay back the bank over several months or years. Just as with credit cards, they must pay interest on the money they borrow. People often take out loans for large purchases. Loans may be used to buy a house or a car.

Another common use of loans is to pay for education. Colleges can cost tens of thousands of dollars per year. Many families are unable to pay so much at once. Students take out large loans to pay for college. They hope their education will lead to a job. Income from a job can help people pay back their loans.

Did You Know?

Going to college can lead to a higher-paying job. But the price of college has been increasing rapidly. In 2013, US college graduates faced an average of $35,200 in debt. This debt can sometimes be avoided. Students can find more affordable colleges. They can apply for scholarships. Earning good grades in high school can lead to scholarships. Students can save money before college. They can also work part-time while in college to help pay for school.

Advantages of Credit Cards

Credit cards have their advantages. You can buy things right away. Credit cards are also safer than carrying cash. If your cash is stolen, it is gone forever. If your card is stolen, you can simply get a new one.

It is important to use credit wisely. This means paying your full debt every month. Using credit wisely builds a good credit history. This is a record of how responsible

If your wallet gets stolen, it is easy to report your credit card as stolen. You can simply get a new card. If the wallet has cash, that money is likely gone forever.

FREE OR DISCOUNTED AIRPLANE FLIGHTS ARE ONE COMMON REWARD OFFERED BY CREDIT CARD COMPANIES.

you are in paying your debts. Credit card companies notice if you have a good credit history. If you pay on time, you may get rewards. These are special benefits for using the card. You may get cash back on some purchases. You may even earn free airline flights.

Be Careful with Credit

Using credit has disadvantages. Banks charge interest on borrowed money. You will end up paying more for things. Credit also makes it easy to overspend. People can quickly build up debt. If they cannot pay it back, interest makes the debt even larger. This makes getting out of

Not being able to see the money you are using can make it easy to overspend with credit cards.

Building up a lot of credit card debt can lead to stress.

debt hard. Imagine a person takes out a loan to buy a car. She has a high-paying job. She thinks it will be easy to make her loan payments each month. Suddenly, she loses her job. She cannot afford the monthly payments. In just a few months, she has a huge debt.

Chapter 2

COSTS OF CREDIT

Using a credit card is not free. Credit cards have costs. One of the biggest costs is interest. Credit card companies charge interest on the money you borrow. They also charge fees. They may charge a fee each year to manage your account. You may have to pay fees if you pay your bill late.

Making sure you have enough money to pay for your credit card purchases is the best way to avoid interest and fees. What kinds of fees might credit card companies charge?

You may see stores that offer small, short-term loans. These are sometimes called payday loans. People go to these places when they need a few hundred dollars or less. Normal banks often do not make such small loans. When the borrower gets a paycheck, he or she pays the money back. Payday loan companies often charge large amounts of interest. They charge much more than normal banks. These businesses are illegal in some places.

Payday loans often involve extremely high interest rates.

Credit card statements help you keep track of your debt.

Statements

Every month credit card companies send statements to their cardholders. These statements may come in the mail. Or they may be sent online. The statement shows account activity during the previous month. One part lists purchases. Another section shows payments made on the account. Finally, the statement shows fees and interest.

The statement adds up the purchases, fees, and interest. Then it subtracts the payments that have already been made. The result is the total amount the cardholder owes. This total is called the balance. The statement shows when a payment is due. It also shows the minimum payment. This is the least amount of money a person can pay without being charged extra fees.

Decision Time

Your older brother is getting a credit card. He shows you the two cards he is considering. One card has a 10 percent interest rate and a $50 annual fee. A second card has a 20 percent interest rate but no annual fee. Which card would you recommend he choose? What are the advantages and disadvantages of each card?

People who use credit wisely pay their full balances every month. Others pay only the minimum payment. The rest of the balance carries over to the next month. Credit card companies charge interest on the balance that carries over. A small purchase can end up costing a lot of money.

Banks also send statements for loans. The statements tell how much you have paid off and how much is left. They also show the interest rate. Like credit card statements, they may show a minimum payment. It is always a good idea to pay loans off as fast as possible. Paying only the minimum gives the interest more time to add up.

One easy way to pay off your balance is to use online banking on a computer, a tablet, or a smartphone.

GROWING INTEREST

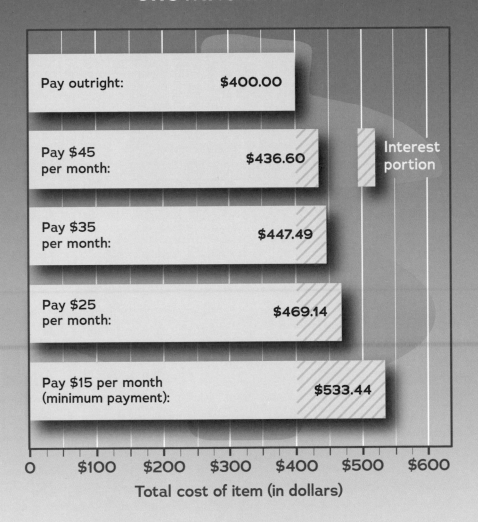

Pay outright: **$400.00**

Pay $45 per month: **$436.60**

Pay $35 per month: **$447.49**

Pay $25 per month: **$469.14**

Pay $15 per month (minimum payment):   **$533.44**

Interest portion

O $100 $200 $300 $400 $500 $600

Total cost of item (in dollars)

This graph shows how cost increases when you take longer to pay your debt. Imagine you want to buy a $400 video game console. If you buy it in cash, it costs $400. If you buy it with a credit card at 20 percent interest, it may cost much more.

Chapter 3

USING CREDIT WISELY

Would you lend money to someone you don't know? You probably wouldn't! You would probably want to know if they are likely to pay you back. Lenders want to know about borrowers before they lend them money. Credit card companies and banks use credit reports to learn about borrowers.

Bank workers called loan officers learn about borrowers before offering them loans. What is one way they learn about borrowers?

Credit Report

When you apply for a card, the credit card company will look at your credit report. This is like a financial report card. It shows how you have paid your debts in the past. It lists any credit and debt you currently have.

Credit users can request to see their reports. It is a good idea to read through your own report to be sure everything is accurate.

Who sees your credit report? Banks use your credit report to determine how risky it is to give you a loan. Employers might look at your credit report before they offer you a job. Landlords may look at credit reports before renting an apartment to you.

There are three large credit-reporting companies in the United States. Each one receives different information about your credit history. They create a report on you the first time you take on debt. Sometimes these reports have mistakes. If you find a mistake, you should contact the credit reporting company. The company can help you fix the error. The problem may be something as simple as a typing error. However, it may also be something more serious, such as identity theft.

Did You Know?

Identity theft happens when someone pretends to be another person. A thief may open up a new credit card under someone else's name. The thief may be able to spend a lot of money before the victim realizes it. The victim may have a difficult time proving the debt is not really his or hers. About 6 percent of the identities stolen in 2013 belonged to people nineteen years old and younger. Thieves may use kids' identities to open credit cards.

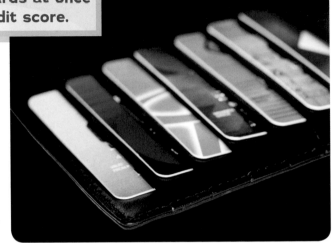

Credit Scores

Many banks use credit scores to decide whether to lend someone money. A credit score on your credit report is like a grade. Sometimes a credit score is called a FICO score. It was named for the credit company that created it. This number tells a lender whether a borrower is a high or a low credit risk. Low-risk borrowers are more likely to pay their debts. Credit scores range from 300 to 850. The higher the score, the lower the risk a borrower is.

Your payment history is part of your credit score. Paying your bills late can lower your credit score. Having a lot of debt brings it down too. Opening too many credit cards can also reduce your score. A lower score will make lenders less likely to let you borrow money.

Using credit responsibly builds a good credit score. You can raise your credit score in several ways.

Borrowers who make payments on time have higher credit scores. You can also improve your score by keeping your debt low. Open new credit cards only when you need them.

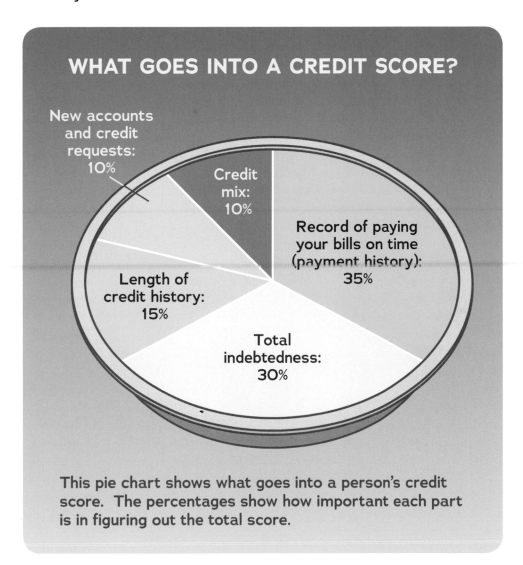

WHAT GOES INTO A CREDIT SCORE?

New accounts and credit requests: 10%

Credit mix: 10%

Record of paying your bills on time (payment history): 35%

Length of credit history: 15%

Total indebtedness: 30%

This pie chart shows what goes into a person's credit score. The percentages show how important each part is in figuring out the total score.

Chapter 4

MANAGING DEBT

The best way to manage debt
is to avoid it in the first place.
Making a plan for spending and
saving can help you avoid trouble!
A budget can help you see how much
money you have
to spend or save.

It's never too early to
start learning about
debt, budgeting, and
bills. What is the best
way to manage debt?

A budget lists all your income and expenses. It can help you spend less. Budgeting makes it easy to create a spending plan. Sticking to a spending plan can be hard. However, it is an important step in staying out of debt. It is a good idea to include savings in your budget. People save for many reasons. Sometimes they save up to buy something specific. They often have an emergency savings account too. This lets them pay for unexpected expenses, such as doctor bills. Having emergency savings means you do not have to rely on credit for these expenses.

Did You Know?

Jude Boudreaux is a financial planner in New Orleans, Louisiana. He has his own way to avoid overspending. Boudreaux created a book with pictures of his financial goals. The book has photos of places he wants to visit. It has pictures of his house, which he wants to pay off in full. Boudreaux flips through the book to remind himself of his savings goals. He says doing this helps him avoid overspending on unneeded things.

Using cash for most things instead of credit is one way to avoid debt.

Credit cards can be tempting. You can get what you want right away. Paying cash may take longer. You have to save until you have enough money. Yet paying with cash can keep you out of debt.

Getting Out of Debt

Most kids are not in debt, but it sometimes happens. What if you accidentally break a vase at your friend's house? You may have to pay for a new one. If you do not have enough money right away, you might pay your friend's parents a little money each month.

ACCIDENTALLY BREAKING THINGS CAN
LEAD TO DEBT, EVEN FOR KIDS.

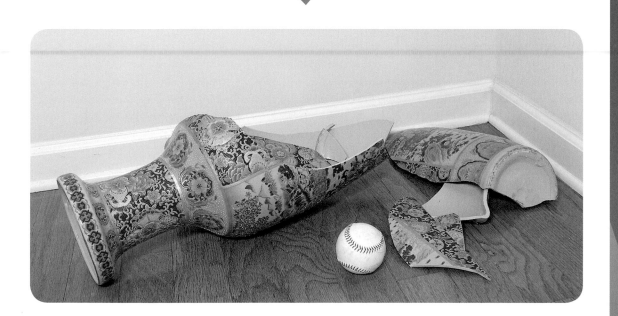

Setting aside money to pay for debts can help you pay them back faster.

Some people find themselves with more debt than they can handle. There are several things you can do to get out of debt. First, make a budget that sets aside money to pay debts. Then think about where you can cut back on spending. Do you really need to buy an ice-cream cone every day? Maybe that money could be used to pay your debt. The faster the debt is paid, the less interest and fewer fees you will owe.

Decision Time

Imagine you owe your mom or dad $50. You borrowed this amount when you went to an amusement park with your friends. You want to make a spending plan that will help you pay the money back. You review how you earn and spend money and see three ways to pay your debt. Which option will you choose? Why?

1. You can save $10 per week by not going to the movies with your friends. If you use that money to repay the loan, you'll pay back your debt in five weeks.
2. Your mom has offered to pay you $25 for babysitting your little brothers on Friday nights. If you agree to do it, you will be able to pay back your debt in two weeks.
3. You usually spend $5 per week on milk shakes. If you skip the shakes, you can pay back your debt in ten weeks.

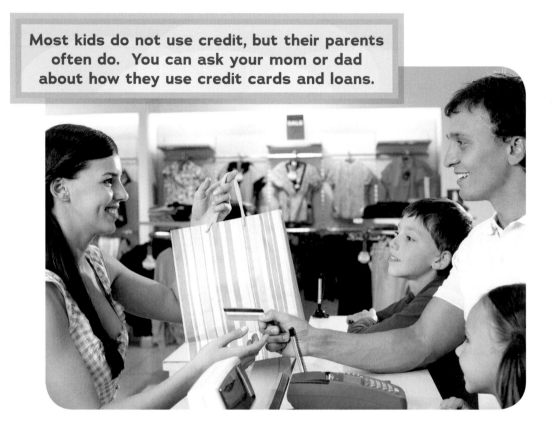

Most kids do not use credit, but their parents often do. You can ask your mom or dad about how they use credit cards and loans.

You can also earn extra money to pay back your debt. See what jobs are available at home and in your neighborhood. Maybe you could earn money by walking dogs or selling lemonade.

It is never too early to be smart about credit. Learn how to budget. Do not spend more than you have. And if you use credit, make sure to use it responsibly. That is the best way to avoid debt problems in the future.

Top Ten Things to Know

1. Credit is not a substitute for cash.

2. Never buy something with a credit card that you cannot afford to buy with cash.

3. Buying something with credit may end up costing you a lot more in the long run.

4. Always pay the full balance on your credit card bill each month.

5. Using credit wisely can help you build a good credit history.

6. Having too much debt can be a negative influence on your credit history.

7. A good credit score can help you get a job, a home, or a loan.

8. It is easy to spend more than you make with credit cards.

9. You can use a monthly budget and a spending plan to help you stay out of debt.

10. Paying off your debt should be a priority that you include in your monthly spending plan.

Glossary

budget: a financial plan that lists all sources of income and expenses

credit: borrowed money

credit score: a number calculated on a person's credit history used to measure how well he or she uses credit

debit card: a card to pay for purchases that uses money from a person's bank account

debt: money owed to another person or organization

identity theft: pretending to be another person in order to steal money or get credit in the victim's name

interest: extra money, usually a percentage, that you have to pay in order to borrow money

spending plan: a list of planned purchases and payments

Learn More about Money

Books

Chatzky, Jean. *Not Your Parents' Money Book: Making, Saving, and Spending Your Own Money.* New York: Simon & Schuster Books for Young Readers, 2010. In this book, a financial expert gives money advice for kids. She includes information about smart shopping and credit cards.

Kemper, Bitsy. *Budgeting, Spending, and Saving.* Minneapolis: Lerner Publications, 2015. Learn how you can spend and save your money smartly.

Sember, Brette McWhorter. *The Everything Kids' Money Book.* Avon, MA: Adams Media, 2008. This book includes information on many different money topics, including how credit cards work.

Websites

Interest: An Introduction
http://www.mathsisfun.com/money/interest.html
Check out this website for more information on how interest works.

Take the Spending Challenge
http://www.themint.org/kids/take-the-spending-challenge.html
Try this game to see how paying with cash or credit can affect how much you owe.

What Is Your Credit Card IQ?
http://www.themint.org/kids/what-is-your-credit-card-iq.html
Test your knowledge about credit cards with this online quiz.

Index

Photo Acknowledgments

The images in this book are used with the permission of: © Jupiterimages/Thinkstock, p. 4; © AVAVA/Shutterstock Images, p. 5; © Photobac/Shutterstock Images, p. 6; © Fuse/Thinkstock, p. 7; © karen roach/Shutterstock Images, p. 8; © Atlaspix/Shutterstock Images, pp. 9, 13, 21, 27, 31, 35; © Diego Cervo/Shutterstock Images, p. 10; © Laura Westlund/Independent Picture Service, pp. 11, 23, 29; © Comstock Images/Stockbyte/Thinkstock, p. 12; © Ammentorp Photography/Shutterstock Images, p. 14; © IM_photo/Shutterstock Images, p. 15; © dean bertoncelj/Shutterstock Images, p. 16; © wavebreakmedia/Shutterstock Images, p. 17; © Blend Images/Shutterstock Images, pp. 18, 34; © Charlie Riedel/AP Images, p. 19; © jason cox/Shutterstock Images, p. 20; © LDprod/Shutterstock Images, p. 22; © Ernest R. Prim/Shutterstock Images, p. 24; © lee seng lee/Shutterstock Images, p. 25; © Mike Stewart/AP Images, p. 26; © Casper1774 Studio/Shutterstock Images, p. 28; © David Sacks/Digital Vision/Thinkstock, p. 30; © Garsya/Shutterstock Images, p. 32; © Pierre Yu/Shutterstock Images, p. 33; © Pressmaster/Shutterstock Images, p. 36.

Front cover: © Stockbyte/Thinkstock (coins); © Laura Westlund/Independent Picture Service (illustration).

Main body text set in Adrianna Regular 14/20.
Typeface provided by Chank.